Day Trading
For Beginners

Become An Intelligent Day Trader-
Learn Day Trading Tools and Tactics, Trading
Psychology and Discipline

I0510645

without contract or any type of guarantee assurance.

The trademarks that are used are without any consent, and the publication of the trademark is without permission or backing by the trademark owner. All trademarks and brands within this book are for clarifying purposes only and are the owned by the owners themselves, not affiliated with this document.

Table of Contents

Introduction

What were you doing in 2008? It might seem like an eternity away for many people, but I remember exactly what I was doing when the Great Financial Crash happened in 2008.

As the fallout from the Lehman Brothers bankruptcy quickly reverberated throughout the US and the global economy, I found myself swept away. Seriously. It was like standing in the middle of a tsunami. My house was suddenly "under water" as its value tanked in the face of relentless court foreclosures that greeted the credit crisis of 2008.

My neighborhood in my corner of the United States was not unique. In fact, the financial devastation that I and my neighbors experienced was all too common. My neighborhood felt like a ghost town as house after house started showing those black and white and red or multicolored signs saying, in so many words, "Bank Owned."

Each sign saying the same familiar story — the former occupant felt that it made more sense to abandon the home's mortgage and surrender the home to the bank for foreclosure than continue to make payments. Who in their right minds would continue to make payments for a $500,000 home when the market value of the house has hit less than $200,000? Who can continue to make mortgage payments in light of all the layoffs happening throughout the United States?

My job disappeared as more and more middle managers saw their companies cut back, if not disappear outright. To say that 2008 was a rough year for both myself and my family would be an understatement indeed. Still, I consider myself one of the lucky ones. I did not lose it all. I still had my optimism.

I still believed, that despite all the financial carnage, that there was a silver lining in that dark cloud overhead pumping out rain. While the rain seemed to be drowning everyone else around me, I had a sense that things are soon going to get better. I was convinced that the world was just going through a rough patch and things would turn out well sooner rather than later.

I was not disappointed

My optimism, as seemingly foolhardy and naive as it was in 2008, was not misplaced. As of this writing, the Dow Jones industrial average has hit record high after record high. The S&P 500 has hit unprecedented levels.

Most telling, the national housing market, which everyone who was supposed to be knowledgeable all but dismissed as crippled for ages, has roared back to life. In fact, in many housing markets in the United States, home prices are now setting new records. That's right, they are beating pre-2008 prices.

I'm happy to report that I did not only witness this amazing turnaround of fortunes, I profited from it. I rode the market back up as it clawed its way from the abyss of 2008. Best of all, I'm no longer dependent on a full time job to take care of my family's needs and ensure all our bills are paid. If anything, 2008's crash woke me up to the tremendous financial benefits of DAY TRADING.

It has become my full time job. "Job" is probably not the right word since I now only work a few hours per day. Regardless, day trading has taken care of all my financial needs and has given me a tremendous amount of freedom.

I can do it while I'm on the sands of Fiji enjoying some tropical blue surf and white sand with my family or at the ski slopes in Switzerland. I can do it anywhere. Also, thanks to limit orders, I can do it whenever. I only need to set my trades and check in later to see how things went.

Day trading, despite my abrupt and desperate introduction to it, has continued to put food on my family's table and give me the peace of mind I never had with a full time job. I believe that the lifestyle it has made possible would benefit people from all over the world. That's why I share with you the raw, basic, beginner's information you need to try your hand at day trading.

Who is This Book For?

This book is not for expert day traders or day traders with tens of thousands of shares traded under their belts. This book is not for people who even have a passing understanding of day trading. Instead, this book is intended for day trading newbies. These are people who look at day trading as a completely new concept. They're curious about it, but they haven't really investigated it in any meaningful way.

If you think that day trading is a new concept and you're motivated to get more information, this book is for you. However, if you have tried your hand at day trading and you've read a few books, this guide is probably going to be too basic for you. I don't mean to turn you off, but I just want to set the right expectations.

This book, once again, is for complete day trading beginners. With that said, it is not intended for stock trading newbies. If you have no clue about stock trading, this book is not for you. However, if you are familiar with trading stocks, but are completely green when it comes to day trading, then this book is for you.

What Will This Book Teach You?

This book aims to give you a clear understanding of what day trading is about and why people do it. This book's goal is to enable you to make an informed decision on day trading, as well as pointing out key tips that would help you make the transition without losing too much money unnecessarily.

Please keep in mind that day trading is highly speculative and the risk of loss is huge. Let's just get that out of the way. If you're a very risk averse person and you're afraid of losing money as you learn how to day trade, day trading is probably not for you. You would be better off looking for something less risky.

Keep in mind that as you try to learn day trading, the chances of you making mistakes will be quite high. Expect to lose money. Instead, focus on earning your "compensation" or "profit" in the form of education. The learning curve is quite high as you make your way through day trading and figure out which stocks to day trade and learning how to interpret signals so you can get out of your position on time.

The good news is, as you get used to the process and as you learn what you need to learn, your success ratio starts going up. Instead of suffering losses day after day, you start turning a profit. How quickly this happens really boils down to how quickly you learn.

Keep in mind that while day trading is very speculative and therefore the risk of loss is huge, it is also true that the potential for great rewards is also high. As the old saying goes: the greater the risk, the greater the reward. Since day trading definitely involves great risks, then you can rest assured that the rewards are definitely there. You're definitely venturing into high reward, high risk territory by trading investments like stocks, options, currencies and commodities as a day trader.

If anything, this book seeks to give you an entry point from which you can use other research resources so you can get the info you need to feel confident enough to start trading. Make no mistake, this book contains enough information for you to start trading, but it also delivers the great benefit of relieving some of the fear and apprehension you may have about day trading.

Chapter 1: What is Day Trading?

Day trading isn't just restricted to stocks. You can day trade currencies, you can day trade commodities as well as options. Day trading involves more of a set of practices that you stick to.

Day trading is the very definition of short term trading. It's all about the short term. In fact, your trading horizon is restricted to one day. This means that you open a position and you close it strictly within one day's trading hours. You engage in it daily, you focus on one or more stocks or one or more commodities or currency pairings or options.

It's important to keep in mind that all your positions are liquidated by the end of the day. Whether you make money or not, you are out of your position by the end of the day. That is the key definition of day trading.

Depending on how much risk you want to undertake, you can also trade using margin accounts. A lot of day traders use margin accounts because they want to trade in volume. If you were going to trade only the money that you have on hand in your account, it probably will take a while for you to earn the kind of daily profits that drew you to day trading in the first place.

People who make north of $5,000 to $10,000 a day are trading on margin. They would have to borrow a certain percentage of their total investment assets to be able to afford to buy or sell stocks that would generate that much profit. To professional day traders, margin accounts come naturally because large volumes amplify profit created when stocks make small percentage moves.

Keep in mind that since you are focused on a quick in and out movement in securities, you're not really looking for massive swings in a stock's value. You are not looking for a breakout 10% game, for example. Instead, it's not uncommon for day traders to exit a position even if the stocks that they're trading move only a fraction of a percent or 1% to 2%. The reason why they are able to do this is because they are so leveraged that even if the stock makes a very small percentage or move, they are trading so many shares of that stock that the small percentage move translates to a decent daily income.

Small Moves for Small Gains

Generally speaking, day traders look for small gains per share per trade. Again, they are not looking for massive returns like a 50% jump in one day. While that does happen, what usually takes place is that the day trader would be more than happy for half a percent growth either way for the stock that they are trading because they are just looking for a really short time trade. We're talking a trade that takes place within 30 minutes or even within 10 minutes. They just need that small move and then they're quickly out of the stock and then they take on a new position.

Again, since they are dealing with a lot of volume because of leveraged trading, they are able to make these quick in and out moves to produce quite a decent return.

How Day Trading Decisions Are Made

A day trader's decision whether to enter a stock or exit a stock all boils down to the probable movement of the pricing of the stock within the trading period. The trading period can be as short as 5 minutes or less or it can be the whole day. Whatever the case may be, it doesn't exceed the whole day.

The day trader makes some educated guesses as to how the stock will move and enters and exits the positions in the stock not just once, but often many times throughout the day. The main focus of these investment decisions is volatility. In other words, the day trader is excited when a stock crashes or bounces and then crashes.

Day traders make money off volatility. They do not make as much money when the stock is trading sideways for a long time and gradually slopes up. A stock might gain value 10% over the course of a year, but that stock, for all intents and purposes, is off limits to a day trader because the volatility isn't there. They would rather trade a stock that bounces 15% up and down, every single day. That stock has enough internal volatility on a day to day basis for day traders to make quite a bit of money.

What Benefit Do Day Traders Offer to the Market?

In terms of economic benefits, how does day trading benefit stock trading as a whole? Well, if anything, day traders provide liquidity to the stock market. They offer a ready base of buyers and sellers of stock. This provides the necessary movement of a stock's price that may encourage other traders to look at either the short term or long term value and prospects of the stock. In other words, by providing action on a strictly short term basis, day traders tend to shine a light on the overall attractiveness of a stock.

Keep in mind this is quite ironic because day traders, as a rule, do not look at the fundamentals of a stock. They don't look at the price/earnings ratio or P/E. They don't look at long term value, they don't look at industry positioning. They couldn't care less about any of that. Instead, they focus more on momentum, share movement, share volume and price velocity going either up or down.

Defining Day Trading By Comparison

Oftentimes, the best way to define something is to compare it with something else. I'd like you to have a clearer understanding by presenting you how it stacks up against swing trading. This is another type of trading style.

Day Trading

Day trading uses up to several dozen trades per day. Day traders trade a lot of stocks and they trade a lot of times per day. Their whole point is to generate a small gain. Whether they are selling short so that they can benefit from a stock dipping or buying low and looking to sell high so they make a profit, the name of the game is to end up with a profit per trade-regardless of how small.

Once they hit their short term targets, they exit. Then they wait for another opportunity to take another position in the stock and ride the stock up or down again. They keep repeating this up to several dozen times per day and, depending on the value of their account, they can trade hundreds of thousands of shares every single day. Due to the volume involved, it's easy to see why day traders can make quite a bit of money.

Technical Analysis

Another key defining point for day trading is its heavy emphasis on technical analysis. Technical analysis in this context is defined as data points indicating the momentum of the stock, its volume, as well as its overall movement history.

Day traders base their whole trading decisions on the assumption that historical stock movements are good predictors of the future behavior of the stock's price. While it's easy to see the weakness of this assumption, for the most part, it holds up for a lot of traders. The logical weakness, of course, is just because the past has played out a certain way, it doesn't automatically mean that the future would necessarily conform with its past performance.

Extremely Short Term

I can't emphasize this enough. Day trading begins and ends within one day. Whether you are trading many times or trading only one time, your position is liquidated at the end of the day. Whether you make money or not, you liquidate at the end of the day.

If you don't liquidate at the end of the day, you are not day trading. Maybe you're doing swing trading, maybe you are doing a longer term trading, but you're not doing day trading. Day trading, by definition, is done completely within a trading day. No trades are ever carried over to the next day or several days.

Day Trading is a Career

Seasoned day traders are able to work only a few hours per day. They know the game like the back of their hands so they know how their target stock moves so they can get away with only working a few hours per day. But don't let that fool you. To get to that level, chances are, you probably would have to work over 40 hours a day.

As you're learning the ropes, you need to put in more time. This can involve quite a bit of effort. It's not uncommon for beginner day traders to spend upwards of 80 hours per week as they learn the game.

The big irony is, during that initial learning cycle, a lot of day traders lose money. It is quite an irony that the more time they spend day trading, the higher the likelihood that they would lose money, but that's the price you pay for your learning curve.

The good news is, once you get good at it, it can turn into your primary way of making money. In other words, you no longer have to work a 9 to 5 job. You can work only a few hours per day and generate an income that is at least equal to or even several times more than your previous work.

It's All About the Small Gains Per Day

Another key factor that I need to emphasize when defining day trading is that the focus here is small gains. I cannot emphasize this enough. You're not looking for a $100,000 profit with one trade. You're not looking for a breakout 20% increase in one day. Day traders who know how to play the game profitably, day after day, week after week, month after month and year after year know that it's all about the small gains.

Now, you may be thinking that a 0.5% gain is nothing to write home about, but if your daily trade is worth $500,000 or, with a margin account, several million dollars, that half percent gain can translate to a nice $10,000 to $20,000 daily pay day. Emphasis on the word "daily."

Understand that by focusing on the small gains, you increase the likelihood that you will come out ahead with day trading. That's why most day traders play the game this way. It's all about getting that small fractional increase in price, or fractional dip if you are short trading.

By way of definition, I would like to spend some time comparing day trading to swing trading. This is another way people play the market. I hope by looking at the difference between day trading and swing trading, you can have a fairly clear idea of how day trading works and what's expected of you when you engage in this type of securities trading.

Swing Trading Defined

Swing trading varies tremendously from day trading because very few trades are involved. For example, if you think that the Netflix stock would explode in 6 months because of a new program that they released or a new programming in their online TV shows, you can take positions on Netflix based on how much the stock sinks. You're waiting for it to dip, and then you will buy some stocks and then would wait for another dip and buy some stocks. Eventually, once the stock hits the target price that you anticipated, you start selling the stocks.

All told, these strategic trades don't add up to much. Maybe you would do one trade once a week. You would monitor how the stock is performing and determine whether this dipped low enough for you to scoop up some shares. You then wait for it to recover and then when it dips again, you buy again. In terms of trading instances, you're actually trading a few times. Now, you may be buying up a lot of shares, but in terms of actual trading activity, there's not that much action.

The Ultimate Focus is On Big Moves

The key thing about swing trading, and long term value trading for that matter, is to focus on big moves. Now, with swing trading, the big move has to take place within a fairly short period of time. We're talking about several days or even weeks. Compare this with Warren Buffet style fundamental trading, which is happy with stock appreciation happening over the span of a year or even several years.

While the same general strategy applies, the big difference is the time horizon involved. Swing trading unfolds over several days or even weeks. Compare this with day trading, which requires you to exit your position within the day. So you're not really given much opportunity to wait out the stock as it achieves its full potential.

In fact, day traders really couldn't care less about the full investment potential of the stock. All they care about is whether there's enough momentum and volatility in the stock's price within a single day for them to quickly enter and exit the stock, not just once, but many times, while hopefully generating a profit with each move.

Swing Trading is Not a Career

Generally speaking, people who do swing trading and long term fundamental trading have day jobs. They either manage their stock trades as part of their 401K investment or self directed IRA investment or personal investment. Whatever the case may be, they have other things that they are doing. They don't rely on swing trading for their main source of income. This is why swing trading is mainly done on the side by both pro and non-professional investors.

It's All About Earning Big Enough Gains

The key to swing trading is that you are trading a lot of your time for a big payoff eventually. Now, the big payoff may take weeks, it might even take months, but when you're doing swing trading, you are happy to trade off the amount of time that you spend waiting for the stock to achieve its full midterm value as it swings up, or swings down in case you are selling short.

Swing traders would happily wait as the stock trades sideways for a fairly long period of time until it spikes up or it gradually goes up to achieve its fullest long potential or gradually sinks down to achieve its short selling profit potential.

Chapter 2: Why Should You Day Trade?

Now that you have a fairly clear idea of what day trading is about, the next question that should be on your mind is why any of this should matter to you. Why should you personally get involved with day trading? Here are just some of the common reasons why people day trade instead of doing swing trade or fundamental trading.

Large Profits

Now, keep in mind that if you're really looking for large, breakout profits, it's probably a good idea to be a fundamental trader or a swing trader because the risks there tend to be lower. This is not rocket science because you're essentially just waiting out a stock as it moves to its full profit potential. The problem is a question of timing. It's anybody's guess how long it would take for the stock to "swing" to its profitable trading target range.

When you day trade, on the other hand, you are shooting for small profits per trade. In terms of percentage appreciation, these may seem miniscule. We're talking about less than a percent. However, don't let the small percentage gain per share fool you. Since you're doing dozens of trades per day and you are trading hundreds of thousands of shares per trade, these small gains can add up to large profits. The best part? They are daily profits. This brings me to the next benefit: quick gains.

Fast Income

I don't know what your daily household expenses are, but most American households, in all likelihood, are in fact maintained at a cost of less than $1,000 per day. Put in another way, you can earn $365,000 per year and after we take out taxes, you can still be comfortable.

Most American households would love to have that level of income. Well, what if I told you that you can enjoy that income level and you don't have to wait a ridiculously long period of time? This is the promise and, in the case of some day traders, the reality of day trading.

You can get quick gains from day trading. The reason is quite simple: the daily timeline. The timeline for day trading is day to day, so you don't have to wait long to see if you earned money. Sounds good so far, right? Well, the flip side to this is you don't have to wait long to see if you lost money.

I don't mean to be a joy kill, but when you are just starting out with day trading, chances are quite high that your day will end with a loss. Now, the more you stick with it and the more know the ropes, the higher the chances that you would be able to flip your outcome and come out ahead instead of ending up with a loss.

Unfortunately, everybody's learning curve is different. Some people are able to figure out the gain very quickly and they go from a loss to consistent profit in a fairly short period of time. Others take a little bit longer. So it really all boils down to how much time, attention and focus you want to put into your day trading career.

Highly Flexible Working Arrangement

Personally, this is the aspect of day trading that I love the most. You work on your own terms. As long as you have an internet connection and you are connected to a very fast trading platform, it doesn't really matter where you are on the planet.

You can be on Boracay beach earning $3,000 a day doing day trading. The next day you can be on a plane to Paris, France and still earning the same amount of money. It's a very mobile and portable way to earn money.

Another great advantage is that you can work on your own time. If you have mastered day trading to a certain extent, you can choose to work only a few hours a day. In fact, some expert day traders only work a couple of hours a day.

Work whenever you want, wherever you want on your own terms. What's not to love? This is particularly valuable for parents who would like to spend more time with their children.

Extremely Exciting

If you are an adrenaline junkie, day trading can definitely be attractive to you. It's really an exciting proposition because hundreds of thousands of dollars are on the line every single day. Now, you can adopt certain strategies that would minimize your exposure to great losses, but there can still be quite significant losses involved.

This is precisely why a lot of people are turned on by day trading. There is quite a bit of risk there and it's that chance of loss paired with a chance of great gain that turns on a lot of people.

Let's put it this way, at a typical boring 9 to 5 job, you're just told by your boss to fill out some forms or research stuff on the internet or write some stuff down day after day, week after week. In day trading, every day is different because the trading dynamics vary from day to day. You're obviously still playing with the same stock, but the dynamics shift on a day to day basis. Each day is different from the day before.

One of the Most Common Myths

One of the most common myths about day trading is that it's intended primarily for a small subset of traders who live in fully industrialized countries like the US or UK or similar countries who have Finance college degrees. This is wrong. Even if you're in a developing country, you can still do well with day trading.

The bottom line is that there's no special education involved. You don't have to get a specialized degree just to be able to participate in this type of securities trading. You don't have to have a certain certification just so you can use the tools you need to day trade. Anybody can have access to these.

Now, keep in mind that just because anybody can access day trading tools, it doesn't mean that anybody can do it. Those are two totally different things because while you don't have a special education or a degree, you do need to know what you're doing. In other words, you have to invest in your own learning curve to do well with day trading.

Trading Status

In the world of international stock trading, successful day traders do have a certain status. Make no mistake about it, to become a consistent success at day trading is quite a feat in and of itself. It's definitely not easy. Accordingly, there are lots of people who would love your advice because everybody loves a winner. And when it comes to day trading, consistent winners can be few and far between.

Know the Risks

Now that I've given you a fairly good sampling of why you should do day trading, as a responsible author, I need to also clue you in on the reasons why many people avoid day trading. Pay attention to the risks below. They are all too real. Make sure you weigh them as you decide whether to engage in this type of trading or not.

Extremely Risky

Let me tell you, all the gains that you generate through small incremental gains and many trades can easily be wiped out with just one trade. Seriously. If you don't watch what you're doing, if the stock you're trading takes the wrong direction and you did not take proper precautions, your gains for the day, the week, the month or even the year can be completely vaporized.

This is the reality of day trading. If you don't diversify your trades or if you don't place proper loss limitations on possible losses on your trades, you can end up in the hole financially. This is especially true if you engage in margin trading.

In other words, you're borrowing from your broker so you can place bigger and bigger trades. Not only do you end up losing on your trades, you end up owing your broker a lot of money because you have to liquidate your positions.

Easy Loss

It's easy to think that any gain, regardless of how small, is enough to generate a profit. It's not that easy. Keep in mind that your costs are not limited to the price of the securities you're trading. You also have to factor in research costs. You also have to factor in opportunity costs. Ask yourself, how much is your time worth? If somebody were to pay you an hourly wage, how much would your salary be?

Now, you have to factor this in the profits or losses of the profits you think you're generating with your day trades. It may very well turn out that you're operating at a loss because you could have been making more money working a 9 to 5 job somewhere else.

Also, you need to pay attention to your platform costs. Different trading platforms have different cost structures. If you're not careful, it may seem like you're making money day trading, but when you take out all your costs, you might actually end up with a loss. You have to be as cognizant as possible of all your trading-related costs because they can have a significant impact on your profit-loss calculation.

What makes this all tricky is that this has to be calculated in real time. You can't just eyeball it. You can't just go by your feelings and feel that you're making money when it turns out that you're not making as much money as you thought you were or, worse yet, you're actually operating at a loss.

Calm Markets

Usually, when people talk about the risks associated with the stock market, they usually think about stocks crashing. That's how most people look at stock market losses. Day traders actually look at the situation very differently. Your big problem is not whether the market spikes or crashes. Instead, your big problem is when the market moves sideways.

This is going to be a problem because this means that pretty much a lot of the big stocks are moving sideways and this pushes all other day traders to a smaller and smaller range of stocks to trade. Since everybody's chasing the same day trading opportunities in play with a limited range of issues, it becomes harder and harder to make money.

In fact, the ideal situation for a day trader is when there is a tremendous amount of volatility in the stock. It bounces up and down that the larger the difference between the high point and the low point of the stock, the more attractive the stock becomes because a day trader's ideal situation would be to ride the stock going up, and then ride the stock going down by selling it short, and then repeat the process again. Each fluctuation might yield a small percentage gain, but if you are able to repeat this several dozen times in the course of a day, you can bet that your payday can be quite huge.

Easy to Get Hooked

It's too easy to get hooked on day trading. Now, the problem with being hooked on day trading is when you feel that you have to day trade instead of chasing an opportunity. It's very important to know the difference because a lot of day traders essentially view day trading as gambling.

Gambling becomes very addictive because the payoffs don't happen all the time. When you pull the lever on a slot machine, for example, it's anybody's guess whether all 7s will show up. If the symbols don't show up the right way, you lose your money. It's this erratic reward system that makes gambling so addictive.

The same applies to day trading or stock trading. You might not get the projected return amount that you were hoping for and you might even suffer a loss. If you repeat this randomness for a long enough period of time, it can mirror the same addiction-creating pattern that produces gambling addiction.

Sadly, a lot of day traders go into the day trading game thinking that they are just simply engaged in financial transactions, but they leave the process full blown gambling addicts. They feel that they really can't get their fix with day trading so they graduate to more and more speculative forms of trading. Others ditch it altogether to just play online blackjack or other forms of online gambling.

You Need to Get a Good Accountant

If you're not careful, the IRS or taxing authority in your country can get on your case. Make no mistake about it, day traders can and do make a lot of money. The problem is, day trading involves so many trades done throughout the year that involve losses and profits.

It may seem like there's a clear pattern of profit and loss and things may seem so simple as far as taxation goes, but often times, they only seem simple. When filtered through the right accounting tools, it may turn out that you owe the IRS a lot of money. This is why it's really important to retain a great accountant to ensure you don't run afoul of the IRS as you day trade your way to a lucrative living.

In the beginning, when you're generating a lot of losses, this is really not that big of a problem because a loss is a loss. The IRS is not going to run after you when you generate a loss. It's when you generate profits mixed with losses that you have to be very careful. The worst situation you can find yourself in is for you to essentially lose money while at the same time owing back taxes to the IRS. In that case, you end up losing twice.

Chapter 3: The Basics of Day Trading

Now that you have a broad overview of what's involved in day trading and the general point of day trading, here are the basics of day trading. A lot of this may seem repetitive, however, the reason why they're being repeated is that certain features of day trading play a central role in this form of securities trading.

I really can't emphasize the repeated points enough. If it seems repetitive, you need to take notice of them and understand them thoroughly because they play a central role in day trading.

Keep It Strictly Daily

When you're trading stocks, options, commodities or currencies, it's important to make sure that you enter and leave your position strictly within a day. You're not doing day trading if you leave overnight positions.

The reason why day traders liquidate their position, regardless of whether they made money or not within the day, is because stock valuation can change overnight. If you've ever traded stocks long, you probably notice that sometimes the ending price of a stock is different from its opening price the next day. This is due to after-hours trading as well as options trading. Whatever the case may be, the pricing has changed. And unfortunately, if you're a day trader who leaves your position open past a day, it's very easy for you to be greeted with a loss the following morning.

Stock prices can change value drastically overnight because of the factors you can't anticipate. You're sleeping or you're taking the time off and the price of the stock has changed. It's easy to get stuck with a massive loss when the market opens.

By sticking to a "no overnight" policy, it gives you lots of control regarding the opportunities you can choose to take advantage of. This is crucial to day trading. This may seem simple, but a lot of day traders are actually confronted with a tremendous amount of temptation.

For example, if you bought a stock at, let's say, $8 and during the day it went up to $16, it's very tempting to hang on to that position. At the back of your head, you're thinking that if this stock doubled in price, who's to say that it won't hit $32 the next day?

Accordingly, a lot of day traders let this temptation get the better of them and they end up with a loss when it turns out that the initial pop in the stock price is quickly reversed in after hours trading. When stock holders realize that their stock doubled in price, they then try to lock in their profits.

Accordingly, instead of seeing the stock spike even further, you are greeted with a massive crash because all these sell orders start getting fulfilled at the beginning of the day. Day traders avoid this altogether by simply liquidating their positions. Regardless of whether they made money or not, regardless of whether they are generating a profit or a loss, they have completely exited their positions by the end of the day.

Play Small Changes Up or Down

Day traders are all about small action. In other words, it may seem like an appreciation or a decrease of 0.5% is insignificant. After all, if a $10 stock goes up in value by 5 cents, it may seem miniscule. It might seem even laughable. However, that 0.5% percent increase might actually translate to a large payday if you have thousands of shares that you are trading.

The whole point of day trading is to stick to small gains, lock them in, and use them to build up your investment base to scale up your profits. These small gains can be made regardless of the direction of the stock you're trading. A stock's price can go either way. You can play long and make money when the stock price increases, or you can make money when the stock price dips by selling the stock short.

Day traders play the market both ways. They can play it going up or they can play it going down. In fact, in most cases, experienced day traders ride stocks going up and down. They stick to the stock and then once they feel that the stock has hit a high point or a resistance level, they quickly liquidate and then they take a short position. They then wait for the stock to drop to a support level and then they change position again as they wait for the stock to rise again.

They repeat this many times in the course of a day. In fact, heavy volume day traders tend to do this several dozen times every single day.

Play Quick Changes

Day trades are very quick. In fact, experienced day traders prefer platforms that execute as quickly as possible. They understand that windows of opportunities open and close in the span of a few seconds. This is why it's really important to identify, lock in and liquidate positions during certain price fluctuations.

This quick in and out movement ensures that they capture certain profit events. Again, the profit events don't have to involve the stock going up. Day traders can and do make money when the stock loses value. By selling short, they sell the stock at a high point, and then they buy it back once the stock prices dip down.

Day Traders Make Multiple Trades Over the Same Day

Really experienced day traders are not content with making a few moves every single day. Instead, within the trading day, experienced day traders take advantage of the multiple price fluctuations exhibited by the stock they're trading.

If you've ever looked at a very busy, high volume stock, you would notice that there is a tremendous amount of up and down fluctuations in that stock's price. In fact, in the span of 30 minutes, a very busy stock can actually go up and down in value several times over. Day traders understand this and that's why they're looking for heavy fluctuation in terms of percentage movements. The more pronounced the changes and the more frequent the changes, the more opportunities they have to make money.

Newbie day traders would tend to try to ride the stock up. On the other hand, experienced day traders would try to ride all the fluctuations. This means riding the stock up and down and back again.

While there is no shortage of experienced day traders trading in the shares of multiple companies, if you are just starting out, it's a good idea to keep things simple by reducing your day trade plays to a small list of stocks. In fact, it makes a lot of sense to try to restrict yourself to one volatile stock. Once you master the patterns, you can then diversify the companies that you trade.

It's All About Speed

It's very important to make sure that you are using the right trading platform if you want to do day trading. I hope I have made it abundantly clear that opportunities come and go very quickly. A stock might build up a lot of momentum and you really only have a span of a few minutes, if that, to take advantage of that opportunity.

Accordingly, you cannot wait around using typical broker trading platforms because it can take quite a while for your trade to come through. This also applies to the information that you are getting. If you're getting stock volume and trade information, you need it as close to real time as possible. If you are using a typical online broker, the information that they give you, as far as pricing and volume are concerned, may be too little too late.

You need to use day trader specific trading platforms. These platforms specialize in catering to the needs of day traders. That's why the information that they offer is very fast and their executions are very, very quick.

Also, you have to use a charting software that is as close to real time as possible. This is a specific type of software and the trading platform that you use and must have really fast charting available. Again, day trading is all about being able to spot opportunities quickly. If your charting program is a little bit slow on the draw, you might be missing out on a lot of opportunities. You could try to capture those opportunities, but end up getting in too late and getting burned.

It's All About Small Quick Gains

This might seem repetitive, but it isn't. If you understand what this subheading means, then it should become clear to you that you should not get greedy. Don't expect a 10% gain from just one trade. Instead, just hit your stock's small changes repeatedly over the course of a day.

Now, keep in mind that the small, quick gains might sometimes be interrupted by small losses. That's okay. As long as each movement is small enough, you can weather quite a bit of losses. The key here is to learn the patterns as quickly as possible so that you can start logging more wins than losses.

I don't want to be a downer, but in the beginning, you probably would log more losses than gains. The good news is, by restricting these to small, quick events, your losses can be minimized. So if you set your threshold to 0.5% and you end up with half a dozen losses, that's a 6% loss for the day. That may seem big, but compare that to a much larger disaster if you did not set a maximum loss threshold.

The key here is to set a loss threshold as well as a gain threshold. That way, once you see the pattern, you can then start locking in on the gains. If your hunches turn out wrong, you're protected because you set a limit on the dips that you can take. Your position may dip to a certain level until you exit.

Chapter 4: What You Need To Do To Get Started With Day Trading

In this chapter, I'm going to lay out what you need to do so you can get going with day trading. Again, I suggest that you use this book to just get a broad overview of what day trading is about, why you should do it and the proper psychology you should have. It also should open your eyes to the kind of discipline, as well as money management and tools and tactics that you should be aware of.

Don't hesitate to read more in depth books on all these sub topics, so you can become fully prepared for your first day trade experience. With that said, in terms of a broad overview, what follows are the things that you need to do to get started with day trading.

#1: Invest In the Right Day Trading Infrastructure

Now, if you trade stocks, you can start day trading using your online brokers trading platform. You can do things that way, but let me tell you, day trading is very different from regular trading because with regular trading, you are given the luxury of time. You can wait for the stock's price to swing to such a significant extent before you liquidate your position.

Day trading, on the other hand, restricts you to trades within the day. So you need real time quotations so you can make instant snap decisions whether to enter a position or liquidate it. Accordingly, the optimal day trading infrastructure requires real time securities quotations.

Regardless of whether you are trading options, currencies, stocks or commodities, you need a platform that will tell you the current price of whatever it is you are trading. You don't want to wait for a 2-minute delay. Your window of opportunity might have evaporated by then.

Also, keep in mind that given the huge amount of stocks you will be trading as a day trader, it doesn't make financial sense to go through the regular online broker platform for trades. This can cost you quite a bit of money because your online broker might seem like a discount broker as far as large one-time volume trades go, but if you are a heavy trader placing dozens of trades every single day, these seemingly "small" fees can add up quite a bit. They can burn a hole through your pocket.

Put in another way, since you'll be doing a lot of trades in the span of a day, paying normal broker fees, regardless of how discounted, can add up and can actually wipe out your profits. You need to sign up with a level 2 trading service that not only offers real time communications, real time executions, but also discount trading fees based on volume. This way, when you are making your trades, you don't pay all that much for the actual execution.

It's also important to make sure that your trading platform is connected to the following networks: Instinet, NYSE Arca and SelectNet. You have to make sure that you get instant access to information that you need and you also have instant execution communications. Whether you're buying or selling stocks, the action must take place quickly, otherwise, you might get stuck with a losing position or you might not be able to lock in on an opportunity that presents itself temporarily.

Finally, you also need access to a news service. Now, keep in mind that day traders don't really care about the fundamentals of a stock. They don't really care about the intrinsic value of a stock. Instead, they look at the effects of mass psychology on the price of the publicly traded shares of a company.

Now, if you get instant news that, for example, a biotechnology company has a new drug filing in the pipeline, this can put a tremendous upward pressure on the price of the stock. By the same token, if news comes out that the FDA has rejected the company's drug approval application, this can put a tremendous downward pressure on the stock. You need to be fully aware.

Day traders make money off volatility. Fluctuations create great opportunities for small gains. However, if you don't buy a stock quickly enough, you might get it when is cooling off from its volatile phase and is now just trending sideways. It's harder to make money off 'calm' stocks. Unfortunately, when you use a slow trading platform, you might get into your position precisely at the point that stock has cooled or is about to cool.

The bottom line? If you use a typical online broker platform, the information tends to be slower and you often get delayed quotes. Often times, the trades may be slower. Now, the delay might just be a matter of a few minutes or even a fraction of a minute, but that's still too slow considering how fast you need to move as a day trader.

#2: You Need to Get Enough Capital

How much money do you need to start day trading? Well, keep in mind that if you want to replace your normal income with day trading, you need to start with a minimum capital of around $50,000 to $100,000 per day.

The reason why you need this much capital is because you would need enough cash to be able to buy the stocks of companies that may be priced in the $100 to $500 range. These stocks may have the tremendous amount of institutional attention, trading volume and volatility that you need to make money. Cheaper stocks may not have these factors and it might be harder to make money day trading those stocks. Accordingly, you need to have enough capital to buy up enough shares of these higher priced stocks so that you can make money off small changes.

It's important to understand that, at the very least, the minimum amount of money you need to be a day trader in the United States is $25,000. This is due to an SEC rule change passed in 2001. Before that time, the SEC allowed people to day trade. In other words, they were able to place four or more trades within a 5-day period and they didn't have to keep a certain minimum amount of money in their accounts, unless they're doing margin trading.

In other words, you are borrowing money from your broker. If you are doing margin trading or short trading at that point, you needed a margin account to do short trades.

Well, with the passage of this rule in 2001, even if you're not selling short, as long as you make four or more trades within a 5-day period, the SEC considers you a "pattern day trader." This rule then puts more requirements on broker dealers that facilitate pattern day trading. Accordingly, broker dealers now require people who are doing a tremendous amount of trades to maintain at least $25,000 in equity value in their accounts at any one time.

The bottom line is simple, if you want to do day trading, you have to have at least $25,000 in your account. However, if you want to make significant money quickly, it's a good idea to have at least $50,000 to $100,000 in your account to start.

#3: Get the Right Information

It's very important that before you start day trading that you have the right information about day trading. This might seem pretty basic. In fact, this might seem so common sensical that it's not even worth saying. However, I need to mention this because a lot of people tend to be tripped up when it comes to different types of trading.

A lot of people think that they are day trading, but in reality, they have the mentality of a swing trader or, worse yet, a fundamental trader. Do you see the bad fit there? Do you see how this can lead to disaster?

Make no mistake about it, day trading has nothing to do with the fundamentals or the intrinsic value of the company you are trading. You don't have to worry about price per earnings ratio, market share, industry dominance or whether the company has a lot of competition. All you care about is psychological factors impacting the performance of the stock of the company you are trading. This is the key to day trading. It's all about psychological dynamics and the emotional mood swings of the market or the people trading that particular stock.

Accordingly, day trading doesn't really care about the facts regarding the company. On a factual basis, the company may be a solid company, but it really wouldn't matter because in terms of short term pricing and stock market fluctuation, the company might be rumoured to be in trouble. So regardless of the fact that the company actually is solid, day traders focus on the impact of the rumours on the very short term pricing of the company's stocks.

Extreme Focus on Technical Analysis and Historical Movements

I've already mentioned previously the fundamental weakness behind day trading. If you're a day trader, your whole strategy really boils down to one assumption. The assumption is that past performance is a good indicator of future events.

You and I know that this is not necessarily the case. Just because something has been happening for a long time doesn't necessarily mean that things will continue according to that pattern. Things do change. Still, by and large, this is a good assumption to make, especially if you are trading a stock and monitoring that stock on almost a minute by minute basis.

The day trader is focused on technical analysis. What goes into technical analysis? Well, first of all, you learn to pay attention to the historic movement of the stock's price on a day to day basis.

If you've been doing day trading for a long enough period of time, you would notice that in the span of a day, certain stocks tend to be quite predictable. Either they start out fairly high in the beginning and then they trend downwards the next day and then they repeat the same pattern again, or they may follow an opposite pattern. They may start the day low and then they trend up and then the next day the pattern is repeated.

This is very important because the more predictable the daily fluctuations may be, the higher the likelihood that if you place certain strategic bets on that stock's movement during the day, you can come out ahead.

Day traders also pay attention to share volume. If there is a tremendous amount of shares being bought, but the price is not moving, the stock might be reaching a point where it would break out because the sellers have all been tapped out and all that's left are buyer that are ready, willing and eager to bid up the price of the stock. The opposite is also true.

Based on all these and other information, day traders are seen to project stock price movement. Accordingly, they're very heavy on charting. They pay attention to moving average or relative strength of the stock.

Now, while you are more than welcome to make your own charts, let me tell you, it's a very technical task. You're essentially just converting raw numbers into visuals. It's probably a much better use of your time to avoid making charts altogether and just use a third party charting service like Iqcharts, MotiveWave or OmniTrader.

What Signals Should You Pay Attention To?

Day traders pay attention to the following signals. They pay attention to head and shoulders, pennants, or flags in their charts to predict the direction of the stock either in the near term or the intermediate term.

#4: Get Experience

I've got some bad news for you. This is the part of day trading that can get really expensive really quickly. This is especially true if you want to trade live.

What I mean by that is you just go in there, jump in with both feet, and start day trading real stocks using your real money. The chances of you losing a tremendous amount of money quickly are quite high. Thankfully, there is an alternative.

Due the heavy risk of loss, you should do paper trading at first. Paper trading involves doing simulated trades. A lot of day trading platforms have trade simulation. These are imaginary trades that you make using actual market information, so there's no risk of losing money when you do paper trades.

The good news is that you learn from actual market information. The more you do this, the more you learn from the simulated paper profits that you generate. If you keep this for a long enough period of time, you learn how to spot opportunities and you become familiar with the market dynamics as well as the trading mechanics of placing a trade, limiting your losses, as well as the schedule or pricing patterns of a stock.

As I've mentioned, most trading platforms have a virtual trade option. As long as you have this turned on, you're not trading money on your account. You're not losing money, but you're not making money either.

You use paper trading to achieve two things. First, it's psychological. You get over the intimidation of actually trading. You become acclimated to how the stock moves and how your profits, although they're on paper and imaginary, are affected by your trades. The other benefit that you get is that you see how the process works. So by the time you are ready to make actual trades involving real money, there is no learning curve.

The same order processing that you use for paper trades is the same as live trades. The only difference is that the option "paper trading" is on when you're doing these trades. But by and large, everything else is the same.

The Drawback of Paper Trading

So considering the fact that paper trading shields you from financial losses, isn't it an unqualified blessing? Well, not quite. You have to understand that when you feel that there is no pressure of loss, you tend to behave differently than if there is actual risk involved. Since there's no psychological pressure due to no risk of loss, you tend to be more logical or you can tend to be more reckless. Whatever the case may be, the lesson is the same.

If you want to truly learn day trading, you have to actually do it with real money because this is where real discipline is involved. It's very easy to be "disciplined" when there is really no money involved, but once you're starting to trade with real money, you will then start confronting emotional temptations to either stick to a position longer than needed or to cut quickly because you feel that the stock has fluctuated negatively enough. Sadly, the only way to learn how to truly day trade is to actually do it and subject yourself to the possibility of financial loss.

#5: Get Disciplined

Before you start day trading, it's important to really get disciplined. Let me tell you, it's too easy to get addicted to trading. A lot of day traders lose money not because they made the wrong decision. Often times, they know how to spot an opportunity and how to lock in for a quick profit. That's not the issue. The issue is that they get so addicted to taking action that they often take action for the sake of taking action.

Past a certain point, there's no real game plan involved. They feel that they just need to trade. They end up over-trading and they get squeezed and they lose money.

You need lots of discipline to only trade when the conditions are right. This is how you separate successful day traders from day traders who occasionally get lucky. You have to wait for when conditions are ripe for profit.

The good news with day trading is that if you pick the right stocks, the pricing is so volatile that these conditions for ripe profit flash and disappear repeatedly over a trading day. In fact, if you pick the right stock, these opportunities appear several dozen times.

That's why I insist that you should stick to the iron rules of trading. What I mean by this is that you should give yourself conditions as to when you should enter a position and when you should liquidate it.

Key Rules of Discipline That Minimize Loss

There are certain key rules of day trading discipline that go a long way in helping you minimize your losses. First of all, you need to place stop loss orders to limit your loss to a fixed percentage. Don't wait for the stock to drop even further in anticipation that it will snap back up. It might actually end up doing that, but if you make it a habit to ride a stock that you bought long downwards, you might end up suffering a loss consistently.

Also, you need to close your positions. You need to get the discipline to close your positions based on set conditions. For example, if you have set your profit margin to 2%, stick to 2%. It's very tempting to think that if a stock has a lot of momentum and it broke past 1% very quickly and then it's at 2% now and it looks like it's rocketing to 3% or even 5%, to just hang on.

Again, just like with the stock that's sinking, you can develop a habit of hanging on to a stock for too long. And the stock's upward trajectory, regardless of how fast it may be, might quickly reverse itself.

It's not uncommon for really volatile stocks to go 15% up and down in the span of a few minutes. Your initial euphoria of not cashing out at 2% as the stock reaches 5% can easily turn into crushing disappointment if and when the stock reverses course and plunges 5%. This often only takes minutes to take place.

Finally, you need discipline to not stay in a position overnight. Regardless of whether you made money or not, regardless of how much profit is possible for you, you need to stick to the "no overnight" position rule.

The problem here is not whether you make money or lose money once in a while by breaking or bending the rules. The problem is, when you develop bad habits, it's very hard to get rid of them. And considering the huge amount of money involved, catastrophic losses can easily come your way if you have the wrong day trading habits.

#6: Make Sure You Can Invest the Right Amount of Time

Make no mistake about it, when you are learning how to day trade, it's very easy to spend way over 40 hours preparing to trade or actually doing trades. Keep this is mind.

Please understand that while there are many day traders who only work a few hours per day, they paid their dues. Often times, they racked up thousands, if not hundreds of thousands of dollars in losses to be able to become that good.

So do yourself a big favor and don't assume that just because a lot of expert day traders have gotten their daily routine down to only a few hours that you automatically would enjoy that lifestyle. It doesn't work that way. You have to pay your dues. And this means that you have to spend over 40 hours preparing trades or actually doing trading.

What do you do with those 40+ hours? Very simple. You're constantly monitoring opportunities. This requires a lot of time and focus. You're also reviewing news to identify any psychological impact on the market's mood on the stock that you are trading. Also, gathering supplemental info in like earnings or regulatory news, drug approvals and industry developments, takes time and focus.

Again, you're not really looking for the long term impact of this information. You're not really looking for facts. You're looking primarily for the psychological effect of this information of the traders buying or selling the stock that you're trading. This all requires a tremendous amount of time and focus.

Don't think that day trading is some sort of get rich quick scheme that you just need to know the basics on, try your hand in, and, after a few trial and error sessions, you start making money. I wish it was that easy, but it isn't. You can get lucky, but don't let your lucky streak blind you because real day trading success is paid for by hard experience.

Chapter 5: The 5 Key Day Trading Success Mindsets You Need To Succeed

To succeed in day trading, you not only have to adopt the right strategy, you also have to have the right mindset. Sadly, if you were to study people who succeeded and failed with day trading, a pattern actually becomes very apparent. People who constantly succeed with day trading have certain mindsets that less successful day traders simply don't have or didn't bother to fully develop. Keep the following mindsets in mind and make sure you adopt them if you're serious about succeeding with day trading.

Follow The Script... Not Your Feelings

Please understand that when it comes to day trading, there is no space for emotions. The reason why day trading even exists is because other traders are emotional. If you want to make money off day trading, you cannot approach it on an emotional level.

Opportunities appear to you because other people got emotional. You easily lose those opportunities if you choose to become emotional yourself. You need to follow the script. This means that you set a goal with your trade.

For example, if you're going to be buying Netflix at a certain price point and you decided that you will exit once you hit 0.5% increase or a 1% increase, stick to that. Don't let your emotions get the better of you, especially if the stock rockets past 1% and is heading to 5% and it looks like it's going to hit 10%.

You have to stick to the script. If you said to yourself that you are targeting a 1% gain, exit the stock once it hits the 1% gain. You can then look at the stock trajectory and then determine when to get in again and ride the stock up or down. Regardless, you need to set a goal and stick to it.

Exit the Position. The bottom line is simple, you need to exit your position even if the event that you're expecting to happen doesn't materialize. You have to look at the actual performance of the stock. You have to look at the actual numbers. You can't base your decision to exit or enter a position on your feelings. You have to understand that it doesn't have to feel right for an action to be right.

Limits are What Ensure Rewards

Another key mindset that you really need to adopt is the realization that the limits that you place on yourself are what ensure your rewards. The more you limit yourself and the more you stick to those limits, the more likely your rewards would come. This is why you have to stick to buy and sell limits.

For example, you might have entered a position and you have to limit yourself to a 1% loss or a 1% gain. Stick to that. Don't override it. Be content with the fact that you placed limits on your behavior and allow yourself to be happy with those limits.

This might seem pretty straightforward, but a lot of people struggle with this because at the back of their heads, they feel that they're denying themselves. They feel that they are being left behind because after all, they're restricting themselves to "small gains." But keep in mind that while you are restricting yourself to small upward pops, you're also shielding yourself from catastrophic losses because you will only allow the stock to dip to a certain point before you exit.

It's really important to overcome the notion that you're somehow, some way, missing out. Instead, focus on the big goal ahead, which is to register very small gains spread out over many trades to produce a solid income every day. Don't get all caught up in the temporary emotional rush of a nice, big payoff or the emotional pain of a setback that you experience. Understand that these emotional rushes and setbacks come and go. So get rid of them altogether by sticking to your limits.

Don't Let Your "Losses" Define You

A lot of day traders don't like to feel like they're losers. I can't say I blame them. I mean, nobody likes to feel like a loser. Nobody likes to feel like a failure. But you have to understand that wins and losses are part of the day trading game. You may have put in your best effort, but for some reason or another, things just didn't pan out and you experience a loss for that day.

The way day trading works is that there is often a small difference between a small profit and a small loss. The worst that you can do is to get emotional when you lose out. You might stay in such an

52

emotional state due to a loss earlier in the day that your emotions could get the better of you. What would have been a profitable trade could easily morph into a losing proposition quickly because you let your fear of losing your subsequent trades get the better of you.

Don't become overly emotional when you register a loss for the day or if you lose money on back to back days. Understand that losses do happen. Be at peace with that fact. Accept that fact and move on because if you're just going to think that your whole day trading campaign is a failure because of back to back losses, then this is going to cost emotional disturbance that would constrict your ability to spot opportunities and make money in the future.

Understand that the past is the past. Don't let the past define you. Whether you made money in the past or you lost money, the past is the past. Day trading is all about the here and now. Focus on that.

Avoid the Big Time Mindset

A lot of people think that the only way they could consider themselves successful in day trading is if they exit their positions with a big gain. This is wrong. You have to understand that this runs contrary to the very definition of day trading.

Day trading is all about small, quick, trades that add up to a lot of money. The precise opposite of that is a small number of trades, each of them involving a large chunk of cash. Avoid that big time payoff mindset. If you feel that that's the way you should trade, I suggest that you switch to swing trading or, better yet, fundamental trading.

Day traders operate under a completely different assumption. They focus on successfully locking small profits using low profit percentage targets. There is no space for a "big time" trade here.

But the good news is, consistently raking in low percentage profits can add up to a nice daily income. I'm not talking about weekly income, I'm not talking about monthly payoff, I'm talking about daily. So by focusing on the small, you might end up with a nice, big paycheck at the end of the day.

Chapter 6: The 4 Most Common Day Trading Strategies

Now that you have a clear understanding of how day trading works, keep in mind that expert day traders tend to focus on four common day trading strategies. Please understand that there are more than four strategies. The more you do day trading, the more you will be able to connect the dots and come up with your own personal strategy. The bottom line is that if a particular method works for you, then stick to it. Accordingly, the only limit to the day trading strategies you can use is your imagination; you still need a starting point.

Being a beginner, it makes a lot of sense for you to explore the four common day trading strategies I am going to describe below, and experiment with them. After some time spent fine tuning these strategies, you can come up with a combination, variation, or just your own personal version of one or more of the strategies described below. Again, these are not the only day trading strategies available out there; however, they are the most common. Use these as starting points in coming up with your own personal day trading strategy.

Scalping

Scalping involves selling a stock as soon as it appreciates to the point where you have covered all commission costs, interests, taxes, trading costs, overhead and a small profit margin you've established for yourself on a certain day. Please understand that all these costs, including commissions, interests, trading costs, taxes and overhead are calculated on a day to day basis. Once you have identified the breakeven point, the small profit margin, and the point where your position has covered your small profit margin, you discipline yourself to sell off your position at that point.

It's easy to visualize this technique on the upside; however, take note that it must be paired with an equally quick tendency to sell if your trade loss parameters are triggered. It's easy to look at the price at which you will sell when you take a profit. It takes discipline to also stick to the maximum price decline or slippage that you would tolerate before you sell off your stock.

Now, please understand that this is easier said than done. While you can easily intellectually accept this, when it comes to actual practice, it's very easy to hang on to a stock that looks like its red hot. It's not uncommon even for veteran day traders to hang on for far too long to a stock that seems like its on fire.

For example, if your target point is to sell Netflix at 107 after you've bought it at 105, it's really tempting to hang on to your Netflix position if the stock broke through the 107 price point and is headed to 112. It's very easy to think that it can continue to rise. You need to be disciplined when scalping. Once you hit the target point, sell. You should not care what happens after the target point has been reached. It shouldn't matter one bit to you whether the stock continues to rise, or not. Your main focus should be whether it hit your target selling point so you can then plot your next move.

The same applies when the stock is going in the opposite direction. Once it sinks past your loss threshold, sell the stock. Don't hang on to it hoping against hope that it'll bounce back up. Maybe it will, maybe it won't; it doesn't really matter. What you should focus on is that you stick to your target price point. Otherwise, it's going to be very, very hard for you to make money with day trading. It really will be quite an ordeal for you because you'll be struggling with second guessing yourself. Scalping is not easy. It seems pretty straightforward, but it requires quite a bit of discipline.

Fading

The next common day trading strategy you should know is fading. Keep in mind that stocks tend to appreciate very fast, then they hit a wall. They hit an upward price resistance, and usually the stock doesn't stay there; it starts drifting downwards. In many cases, it drops like a rock.

Day traders know this; that's why they pay attention to two key factors when they're trying to fade a stock. They look at how fast the stock price appreciated, and they pay attention to the volume. What they would do is they would log in a short sale order once the stock has reached the point where its price appreciation has outpaced the volume of trade. This means that the amount of buyers has been pretty much used up, and its only a matter of time until the stock experiences a pullback.

When you sell a stock short, you make money when the stock drops. You borrow shares from your broker platform, and you sell it at a high price. You wait for the stock to drop, and you cover your position by buying back the stock. The difference between the stock price when you sold it, and its price when you bought it or covered it is your profit. This is a very common phenomenon.

Fading is actually more common than most people think. As more shorts appear on the stock, and people who bought that stock long start to adopt the stock, there's tremendous pressure for the stock price to drop. Now, fading can get quite tricky. You have to time it right. You have to understand that once the stock starts dropping, there's going to be an upward price momentum as short sellers start covering their trades. When they cover their trades, they buy their stock back. So this artificial demand created by short sellers covering their short trades puts an upward momentum on the stock price.

You don't want to be the day trader that gets caught in the upswing of a sinking stock. Not surprisingly, a lot of day traders who fade stocks choose target prices that are a percentage point or two below the top price they bought the stock at.

Daily Pivots

After studying the stock's performance from the previous day, day traders would try to lock in on a low entry price. They try to make an educated guess as to where the stock would settle for the day. This is supposed to be the low point of the stock for the day.

They would use data points like the previous day's support level, as well as resistance levels; they would lock in on a low entry price which is usually the projected support level for the stock. They would then wait to ride the stock up until it hits their target resistance level. They would then exit their position and then try to short the stock at the resistance level and ride it down and buy back the stock at the support level.

Beginning day traders probably would have a tough time doing daily pivots. It's probably a good idea if you're just a beginner to ride stocks up instead of trying to ride them down. Do understand that it's actually riskier to short stocks, because if you're buying a stock long, and it crashes, the stock only has so far to drop until it hits zero.

Theoretically speaking, the opposite isn't true. If you're shorting a stock, the sky's the limit as to how far the stock can appreciate in value. I hope you can see the difference, and I hope you can see the risk in short selling stock. Still, in the hands of capable and experienced day traders, daily pivots can become quite lucrative.

Momentum Trading

Momentum trading is especially dependent on the quality of your charting and real time tracking tools. You buy a stock when it's increasing in price. Matched with increasing stock trade volumes, you then sell the stock when it starts reversing momentum. In other words, you are buying the stock not because of its intrinsic value, or its industry position; you're buying it because a lot of people are buying. You're buying it because there's a lot of market interest in that stock. You then dump the stock once it reaches its peak market interest.

This sounds pretty basic on paper, but it's actually very tricky. Traders must be disciplined enough to close at the start of the trend reversal. Understand that all stocks go through trends within the day and oftentimes, they go through several trends in one day.

You have to be disciplined enough to close your position out at the start of the trend reversal. The moment the momentum stops, or experiences a resistance, you exit. You can then choose to ride the stock back down, or you can wait until the momentum picks up again. Regardless, you need to exit. What makes this tricky is you need to leave the stock, regardless whether you earned a profit or not.

Before you continue reading further, I would like to know if you are enjoying reading this book and find it valuable. If so, would you be kind enough to _leave a review for this book on Amazon_? It'd be greatly appreciated!

Leaving review only takes a few seconds and it will enable me to continue to produce high quality, enriching content to serve people like you.

Chapter 7: Getting Started With Day Trading

To get started on your day trading career, you need to do the following:

Get your research together

Read this book and get familiar with the concepts explored in this book. I need you to drill down further, and research topics that you learn about in this book. The more you drill down, the better.

However, keep in mind that you don't want to get stuck in analysis paralysis. People who are suffering from analysis paralysis think that they need to read book after book and do extensive research until they get all the information they need to make the right move. I'm sorry to be the one to tell this to you, but you'll never get to that point.

There has to be a point where you have to stop researching and start doing. While it's obvious that there's a lot of risk involved in day trading, you can minimize that risk only up to a certain extent with research. Eventually, you have to make that leap of faith where you're actually doing day trading and learning from experience.

Once you actually do day trading, you would then be able to connect the dots and come up with your own personal strategies for minimizing losses and maximizing your gains. Research can only take you so far. While it's important to get your research together and drill down, you need to know when to draw the line and make that leap from research to actual action.

Start paper trading

The good news about taking action is that you don't have to take action that would necessarily subject you to the risk of financial loss. Once you've gotten your research together, start paper trading.

Find platforms that allow you to make simulated trades. These are imaginary trades using real market information. What you're doing is that you're familiarizing yourself with how the trading platform works and, most importantly, getting over the emotional intimidation of actually doing day trading. What makes paper trading tricky is that you have to fight the natural tendency to want to jump in with both feet.

I know that you would want to start making real money. I know that you want to tap the full potential of day trading. However, you need to pay your dues first. You need to invest as much time as you can into paper trading to give yourself enough time to know the ins and outs of day trading. This increases your level of confidence. It also enables you to become aware of certain decision process patterns that you tend to follow. By knowing this information, you can position yourself to become a better day trader. You can build on your strengths and work on your weaknesses.

Unfortunately, it's very easy to lose money when you go straight from doing research to actually doing day trading. You have to follow a sequence of steps. Start paper trading, start it early, and put in the time.

Put in the time

Stick to paper trading until you have a good idea of the techniques involved. Chapter 6 is a good place to start. Pay attention to the different strategies; try them out using risk-free paper trading. Keep at it until your win/loss ratio is solid.

I don't mean to be a spoiler here, but let me tell you: in the beginning, you're going to be losing more than you would win. That's okay, because you're not losing real money. You have to put in the time and practice day trading day in day out until your win/loss ratio improves. Once it becomes solid, you know you are getting close to getting ready to doing actual cash trades.

Get your cash together

This might seem like step 4, but this step should actually be done at the same time as step 1. At the same time, you're doing research, as well as going through the subsequent steps like paper trading and putting in the time for paper trading.

You should start gathering cash. Make sure you have enough cash to trade at a scale that would at least give you a good chance of making a nice daily income. If your target is to earn $1,000 after taxes, then you need to have a nice starting base. We're talking at least $25,000 to $50,000. A lot of expert day traders recommend that newbies start with $50,000 to $100,000. This capital level ensures that you would be able to trade more expensive stocks that have the volatility and market volume that you need for profitable day trading.

Sign up for a level 2 account

Look for a level 2 trading account offered by online brokerages or platforms that specialize in day trading. It's very important to make sure that you use an integrated trading platform. By integrated, I mean you use a platform that not only enables you to trade in real time so you can lock in on fast developing opportunities, but it should also have sophisticated charting software bundled in.

Thankfully, there's no shortage of such level 2 accounts. Of course, you need to experiment with the different charting programs so you can see which one you can understand most easily and use most frequently. You have to insist on multiple functionalities from the same platform. The platform must be able to execute trades quickly. It should also give you access to real-time quotes and help you chart the stock that you're trading.

Sign up for stock news services

As I have mentioned previously, day trading is really all about psychology; you're trading on market psychology. You're not trading on fundamental value of the stock; you're not focused on the intrinsic worth of the stock both now as well as in the future. Your focus is whether there is enough market attention in the stock that would produce volatility.

Unlike value investing, or swing trading, your primary focus is not on the stability of the stock over time, but on its volatility. The more volatile the stock, the better. However, you have to pair it with a tremendous amount of volume, as well as, market attention. Accordingly, you need to sign up for a stock news service that would give you late breaking news regarding that stock.

Once you are aware of the news that's being circulated about that stock, you can then make educated guesses as to the psychological effect of that news. Now that news doesn't actually have to be factual, it can involve rumors. The focus is not on facts, the focus should be on the effect of rumors or market impressions and moods on the stock that you're trading. This is where real time stock news services come in really handy. Now, you can buy this as a separate service, or you can sign up for it as part of an integrated trading platform.

Start trading small

Once you're ready to go from paper trading to actual cash trades, don't jump in with both feet. Seriously, you're going to get burned if you do that. Try to stick your toe first in the water. Do this for a few weeks. If you're able to handle it, do it for a few months.

The key here is to get acclimated real life trading. As you will soon see, it's going to be very different from paper trading. When you're doing paper trades at the back of your head, you know that you're not going to lose money, you know that if you make a wrong call on the stock, and it goes south instead of going north, you're not out of any of your hard-earned cash.

When you do live trades, on the other hand, the risk of loss may seem subtle at first, but it may start distorting the quality of your decisions. This is why you need to acclimate yourself slowly and surely through live trading. Start trading small, start with very conservative profit margins. In fact, I would strongly suggest that you calculate your exit prices based on your breakeven point. In other words, you're not even looking to earn money; you're just looking to cover your taxes, and your costs. Keep it at that level until you become confident with your ability to establish a solid win/loss ratio.

Chapter 8: Any Victory is Still a Victory

The key psychology to successful day trading really boils down to discipline. A lot of day traders would have been a lot more successful if they understood that any victory is still a victory. The problem with most people is that while they can intellectually understand the idea of accepting a small percentage gain goal at the beginning and sticking to it, eventually they get cocky, seriously.

As they make solid calls day in day out, they start wondering to themselves: "I know when to make the right calls. I know how to make the right decisions. My trades come out right. Why am I denying myself of the great success that I'm otherwise capable of achieving?"

So, their discipline starts to slip. In the beginning, they would be perfectly happy with half a percentage gain. Then they would try to scale that up to 1%, then to 2%, after a certain point, they just go crazy and remove all limits, and they wait to ride out the stock to its highest level of appreciation. At that point, they are no longer day trading, because at that point, chances are, they're going to have to wait several days or even weeks to even reach the fullest potential price for that stock.

Assuming that it even continues to go in a positive direction, you have to avoid this, because if you want to become a day trader, you have to set a percentage gain goal and stick to it. Don't ask for more, don't settle for less. As long as the stock hits that percentage gain goal, you hit the exit. Nice and simple.

Keep in mind the Big Picture

Understand that success in day trading really boils down to success in discipline. Discipline is like a muscle; the more you practice discipline, the better you get at it. You are able to withstand greater and greater levels of temptation. Believe me, when it comes to day trading, you'll be tempted sorely, seriously.

You will be subjected to all sorts of conflicting emotions. You have to keep your eyes on the big picture. The big picture is simple, small consistent gains every single day win out over one-time gains followed by many losses. What's the point of racking up $100,000 dollars in a day when ultimately, it's going to be followed by several months of solid losses? It doesn't make any sense.

So focus on small consistent gains. Pay attention to your ability to connect the dots. Keep your eyes open to the patterns that you become aware of, and consistently push yourself to become more and more aware of the different patterns and trends of the stock that you're trading. If you allow yourself to be content with small consistent gains, plus the experience you're getting, you may be in for a very big payday in the future. The best part to all of this is the payday comes every single day and its more or less consistent. The key is whether you would allow yourself to reach that point. It takes quite a bit of self-discipline and self-control to get there.

Don't let your ego get in the way

I know I sound repetitive, but the reason why I'm repeating this is because I've seen otherwise successful day traders crash and burn because they let their ego get in the way.

Let's face it, day trading is not a science. It doesn't matter how many hyped up books on day trading you've been exposed to, or how many ads you've read that claim to take the guesswork out of day trading. The simple truth is day trading is an art, and just like any art, in many cases, despite your best efforts, you're going to end up with the wrong end of the trade. The key here is to not let your ego get in the way. You're not a loser if you lose out several days back to back. Even if your past 30 days' worth of trades all ended up in losses, it doesn't necessarily mean you're a loser.

If you start looking at your activities in black-and-white terms, in the simplistic division of winning and losing, it's too easy to define yourself based on past performance. Furthermore, it's also easy to fall in the trap of wanting to vindicate yourself by trying to "win big" one time. You end up overtrading, and at best, you settle for cents of the dollar, at worst, you end up suffering loss after loss.

Don't make things worse on yourself by letting your ego get its way. Everybody suffers setbacks. This happens to even the most successful day traders. What's important is that you focus your attention on the key lessons you've learned from your setbacks.

Chapter 9: Scale Up with Margin Trading

Warning: Do not implement this until you have reached a nice win/loss ratio. Let me repeat: do not implement the information found in this chapter until you have taken care of your win/loss ratio.

You should probably already know that to get your win/loss ratio into shape, you really have to do a lot of training. I suggest that you really take your time with paper trading. There's no risk of loss, and you can go a long way in training yourself in determining the patterns that work best for you. Keep in mind that trading patterns that work well for other people who make a lot of money may not necessarily work for you. Everybody has to find their own way. The worst part to all of this is that you will only learn how to do this by actually doing it. There's really no other way around it.

Using risk-free paper trading is a great help. However, you need to take the training wheels off, so to speak, and do real trades to get the real hang of real time trading. With real trading, the stress is real. With real trading, the pressure is real. You can start small, and then you can start scaling up once you have reached a win/loss ratio that you can be happy with. Only after you've reached that point should you even entertain thoughts of scaling up the amount of money you are working with.

Let's get one thing clear; margin trading enables you to borrow a large chunk of money from your trading platform. This can be a great blessing; it can also be a terrible curse. It all boils down to whether you are trading confidently, and whether you know what you're doing. This is why I really caution people to be very careful when it comes to margin trading.

I'm not saying that they should avoid it. I'm not saying that they should not consider it as an option, instead they should use it for its intended purpose: it's a tool for scaling up your gains. That's all it is. It's not free money. It's not a special magical weapon that you would use to make all this amazing money overnight. It's none of that. It's just a specific tool that you use to leverage the assets that you have so you can scale up your gains. Used properly, you can earn more money faster. Follow the sequence below.

Start with paper trading

It's really important to make sure that you start with paper trading. It's risk free, and it gives you a tremendous opportunity to learn what you need to learn so you can get your win/loss ratio in proper shape. Your win/loss ratio is your report card; you need to keep referring to it to properly know when you are ready to actually invest with real money. It's very important to track your strategies when you're doing paper trading. You're not just jumping in there and making some random trades, and following your feelings and hoping to get lucky; that's not the strategy. Simply rolling the dice, crossing your fingers and hoping for the best does not make consistent millions. Sorry, it just doesn't work that way.

You have to pay attention to what you're doing and look for patterns. Try to connect the dots. What timeframe tends to make more money for you? What trading strategies tend to make more money for you?

Identify your weaknesses and build on your strengths. Come up with your own personal strategy using real stock information made possible by paper trading. Given enough time and attention to detail, you'd be able to come up with truly winning strategies that would increase your win/loss ratio. Once you are very confident about your ability to consistently gain, then you're ready for the next step: cash only trading.

Starting with cash trading

Let's get one thing clear here, once your hard earned cash is on the line, the pressure really begins. It's easy to get excited about paper trading, but ultimately at the back of your head, you know that there is no real risk involved. You're not out of pocket when you make a wrong call. With cash trading, your hard-earned money could go up in smoke quickly if you make mistake after mistake. Accordingly, it pays to be really cautious.

I'm not saying that you should be completely gun shy. I'm not saying that you should trade in tiny amounts. Instead, start with a small enough amount of cash which still places a lot of pressure on you. This is kind of an awkward balancing trick, but you need to find that intersection between the amount of risk that you are comfortable with, and the amount of pressure that you need to really pay attention to what you're doing.

Start at that level and start making trades. Document what you're doing. It doesn't have to be extensive documentation. You don't have to come up with tons of pages of in-depth reports as to what you're doing. Just come up with something that is clear enough for you to refer to so you can see what you're doing right and what needs improvement.

Start scaling up with your cash trades as your profit and loss ratio improves. Again, I can't emphasize this enough, when you're beginning to trade in cash, expect losses. That's just the nature of the beast. Get emotional ready for it. However, if you stick to it, and you're paying attention to what you're doing, and scaling up properly, eventually, your profit loss ratio will improve.

Start scaling once your profit/loss ratio allows it

You can start scaling up using your margin account in a very significant way once your profit/loss record is positive enough to allow it. The key phrase here is "positive enough." Sadly, this threshold varies from person to person. It all depends on your appetite for risk. Some people insist on a 95% profit/loss ratio. Others are so risk tolerant that they're okay with a 50/50 ratio. There's really no right or wrong answer. You're the only person who can truly know what the right profit/loss ratio is.

It all boils down to your comfort level. It all boils down to how confident you are in bouncing back when you encounter turbulence, or experience a setback. Keep in mind that day trading is very risky, and to offset that, you need handsome returns. Unfortunately, without the scale of margin trading, it takes a long time to get to that amount of cash that you can use to get the type of returns that would handle the risk that you're undertaking.

Remember: you're scaling for opportunities, not just to make more money

Another important factor to keep in mind here is that scaling up through margin trading doesn't just give you more capital to work with. The greater return in terms of absolute cash is a good thing, but there is a bigger benefit to scaling up through margin trading.

You have to understand that the more cash you have to work with, the more confident you can be in entering and exiting a position even with minuscule movements. Let me repeat that. When you have a lot of cash, you can successfully earn quite a bit of money even with microscopic movements of the stock you are trading; this is due to scale.

If you only have a thousand dollars, and you're trading a $100 stock, that stock has to move quite a bit for you to earn decent money. Now, compare that situation if you're working with a million dollars. If a stock just moved half a percent, you would make a lot more money in terms of absolute dollars with a million dollar investment than if you had a $10,000 investment. You see how this works?

It's important to understand that you are scaling for opportunities primarily. You're not just looking to making a lot more money, because you have a lot more money to work with. In fact, if that's your attitude, it can be quite detrimental to your trading success. How come? Focusing too much on the money can push you to overtrade. This is a big danger. A lot of otherwise successful day traders tend to settle for cents on the dollar because they tend to overtrade. When they trade more often than they need to, they increase their chances of loss.

Chapter 10: Pace Yourself Right

Keep in mind that successful day trading is a risk. It's a marathon; it's never a sprint. For the life of me, I've never seen a fellow trader just start making millions of dollars right out of the gate. Oftentimes, I see people who are in a rush to make a tremendous amount of money fall flat on their face. You have to pace yourself right; what you're really engaged in is a race with yourself. You're not competing with other investors that you hang out with. You're not competing with legendary day traders that you've heard of. You're competing with yourself.

Your primary challenge is to overcome your lack of discipline. Your primary challenge is to learn what you need to learn so you can achieve success. This can be quite difficult for a lot of people. Let's face it, we all prefer the path of least resistance. We would prefer shortcuts. If given the choice between the quick and easy way to make a lot of money, and the long, harder and disciplined way, most people would pick the shortcut; that's just human nature.

But you need to resist that and pace yourself right. Don't be in a hurry to earn $1,000 a day. If anything, look at the lessons you're learning as your primary form of compensation as you seek to educate yourself in the intricacies of day trading.

Focus on learning first

By making your day trading education your first priority, you should be ready, willing and eager to day trade only to break even; that should be your first priority. Consider it a victory when you break even. Why?

You're looking to learn, you're looking to connect the dots, you're looking to see the common patterns that play out day after day on the stock you are tracking. The sooner you discover these patterns, the sooner you can start working towards your target daily income. Experience should be your first payoff.

I know that this rubs a lot of people the wrong way because, hey let's face it, the main reason you're even reading this book is because you have probably heard that you can make thousands upon thousands of dollars every single day doing day trading. You probably also heard that you only need to work a couple of hours a day at that to earn that kind of income. While that is true, it takes a lot of trial and error and, yes, losses to get to that point.

You have to understand that with any kind of investment, it's very easy to get blinded by the "survivor effect." Look at any human endeavor and its easy to see the effect in action. In other words, when you look at sports for example, it's easy to get the impression that all boxers are strong, quick and successful. The problem is you're only looking at the winners. Even the guys who get beaten after one round, are winners because they have beaten other guys to get to that level. You see how this works?

So by only allowing yourself to look at the successes, you get a distorted view of the general process behind the success that you're seeing. Success is paid for, by and large, by failure. I'm not trying to discourage you, instead I'm trying to open your eyes to the fact that you have to insist on experience as your payoff as you make your way to the level of success you have in mind.

Track how disciplined you are when you trade

I can't recommend tracking enough. You need to use some kind of documentation so you can clearly identify the things that you're doing right. In addition to this, you should also take notes on how disciplined you are when you trade. Take note of your emotions. Take note of your thinking processes.

Now, you don't necessarily have to write a novel about this. You don't have to write some sort of long convoluted description; you can make short notes. Still, when you look at your notes, you should be able to track your emotional state so this can help you achieve the right disciplined mindset to maintain your cool.

You have to remember that day trading and playing poker actually share many similarities. One common similarity is that it's all really about mastering your emotions. The other players might be raising the stakes, but if you let it get to you, you might end up being pushed into making the wrong decision and this can lead to catastrophic results.

Stand as slowly and for as long as you can

I know you want to make a lot of money sooner rather than later. However, do yourself a big favor and stay on the slow lane. In fact, you should stay on it for as long as you possibly can. Learn as much as you can, identify as many patterns and most importantly, learn as much about yourself as you day trade. If you're able to do all of these, then you will be positioning yourself for great success later on.

Chapter 11: From Mere Income Generation to Vocation

Look at day trading not as some desperate dash for cash. People who need cash yesterday should not even think about day trading, seriously. Close this book, and look for a job. I can't emphasize that enough.

If you are in dire straits, you shouldn't be looking for quick cash online. You shouldn't look at day trading as a quick solution to all your financial problems. That's a recipe for financial disaster. If you think you're in a hole now, it's going to get worse. Let's face it, if you do things out of desperation, you will attract failure; that's just the way it works. You're not thinking clearly. You're focusing on what you're losing, and you often lose sight of the big picture.

You need to have the right mindset, and you have to understand that day trading is not just income generation. While it does a good job of providing solid income to a lot of people from all four corners of the globe, it's actually more than that. It's a vocation; it's a calling. I consider it an adventure because every single day is different from the day that came before.

Also, every single day, I'm given a tremendous opportunity, not to only learn about the psychology of the market, as evidenced in the up and down flow of the stocks I'm trading, I also learn about myself. I learn about my emotional states. I learn about my triggers, and all of this personal discovery is very exciting to me. I'm driven primarily by the thirst of learning something new.

You should adopt something similar. Focus on the adventure, focus on how you change and improve over time. Make no mistake about it, day trading is going to challenge you. It's going to challenge your level of self discipline, your ability to control your impulses, and it also tests your goal-setting effectiveness. Instead of looking at these as hassles or problems that you need to overcome so you could reach a big payday, look at these as rewards in themselves.

Being more disciplined is a good thing. Being able to control your emotions is a tremendous asset. Learning how to set goals in such a way that you have a higher likelihood of becoming a reality is a great skill to have. Focus on these instead of the money. Now, I'm not saying that you should absolutely disregard the income generation aspect of day trading, but my point is that there are other important considerations to keep in mind. These are of equal if not greater importance.

Stay passionate

Again, you can't look at day trading with a desperate mindset. From my many years of experience living on this planet, I've learned that the more desperate I am to achieve some sort of result, the less likely that result will come to pass. Desperation seems to repel success.

What's the opposite of desperation? The answer is simple: passion. When you're passionate, you're curious. When you're passionate, you're in love with what you're doing; every little revelation excites you. It's not about your emotions per se; it's about your inner need to take things to the next level. Learn the patterns. Focus on your most successful moves. If you're able to do this in light of the discipline that you're building, you can convert "lucky trades" to predictable trades. This is the real mark of expertise.

Day traders who make a consistent income from day trading have gone past simply getting lucky to predictably producing results. Now, per trade, the results may not be all that impressive, but given the scale at which they trade, it's easy to see why they make tens of thousands, if not hundreds of thousands every single day. The good news is if they can do it, so can you.

Conclusion

Successful day trading is a journey; it's not a destination. In this journey, you're going to change. In this journey, you're going to be challenged. Your level of discipline, self control, and your ability to look at the big picture over a long period of time are going to be tested. Accordingly, you need to look at the tools and tactics that I've mentioned in this book to help you get a proper context for day trading. Ultimately, it's your mindset that will determine if you'll be a successful day trader or not.

While it's easy to look at day trading success as a simple matter of failing or succeeding, it's not that simple. The vast majority of day traders are actually in the middle. They haven't completely failed, but they haven't succeeded either. They're just treading water; they're settling on cents on the dollar.

This is too bad because by simply adopting the right psychology, which leads to increased level of discipline, you'll be able to have a broad view of day trading. This broad view would enable you to scale up properly and employ the right tactics so you can go from simply being lucky from time to time to consistently getting the results that you came for.

I wish you the greatest trading success.

Finally, if you enjoyed this book and received value out of it then I'd like to ask you for a favor. Would you be kind enough to *leave a review for this book on Amazon*? It'd be greatly appreciated!

Other Useful Resources

I believe this book shared you all the necessary information you needed to understand Day Trading better and apply these principles in order to be an intelligent day trader. The next step is to implement what you have learnt.

Would you like to read **my other two books** which I have written to help newbie investors like you?

1. *Stock Market Investing For Beginners,*

2. *Investing For Beginners*

You worked hard for your savings. Don't let inflation eat up your savings' value. Read these books and start on the ROAD TO FINANCIAL FREEDOM AND ABUNDANCE.

Previews of both books are available on following pages.....

Preview of

<u>Stock Market Investing</u>
<u>For Beginners</u>

Simple Stock Investing Guide To Become An Intelligent Investor And Make Money In Stocks

By David Morales

<u>Available on Amazon</u>

<u>*https://www.amazon.com/dp/1544770812*</u>

<u>*https://www.amazon.co.uk/dp/1544770812*</u>

Introduction

This is my personal stock trading story: I started trading stocks when I got my first part time job while I was still in college. You might think that this was a pretty great start. After all, most people never really start stock investing until they are already established in their careers. In fact, the average American trades stock primarily as a passive investor as part of that person's 401k plan at work. Put simply, most people don't actively look to invest in stocks.

You might think that I had a great early start with investing. Well, not quite. While Microsoft, Apple, Cisco and other amazing companies were trading at the time I started investing in stocks, I didn't invest in those stocks. If I did, I'd be worth hundreds of millions of dollars today. In fact, when I started investing, Cisco, Apple and Microsoft were trading at very low prices.

What I did was I just dove into stock investing and bought whatever "cheap" companies were being recommended by investment "experts" featured in the newspapers I read at that time. I only paid attention to two factors: the price of the stock and where it was in its 52 week valuation. If the stock was trading near its 52 week low, and the stock was affordable as far as my budget was concerned, I bought the stock.

I did not look into its industry, I did not do research regarding the company's market position. In many cases, I didn't even know if the company was making any money. I only looked at whether it was recommended by experts and whether it was cheap enough. Every pay check I would set aside a few hundred dollars to buy these "cheap" stocks I was told had a "tremendous upside."

As I mentioned, I didn't bother to do thorough industry research, nor did I pay attention to the stock's momentum, volume and other crucial trading details. The result? Of the 5 companies I invested in, 2 went bankrupt. One is still around, but it's a dormant "shell" company that is a penny stock. To make matters worse, it barely trades. The other two companies that I bought, I ended up selling them for prices that were lower than I bought them for.

Fast Forward to Today

Now, I make money on all my trades. I know when to buy in, and I know when to sell. In fact, it has become quite predictable to me. While I don't always rack up daily profits in the 5 digit range, I definitely have come a very long way from when I began trading. I actually make a profit every single day.

I've got some great news for you: if I can go from a hype-crazed foolish investor throwing good money after bad on lousy stocks to someone who can reliably pick winning stocks, so can you. The only difference between you and me is information.

This book spells out the information you need to begin your stock trading career the right way. Don't begin it the same way I did. I lost money. I worked hard for that money while I was going to college and all that money just went up in smoke. Learn from my mistakes.

Indeed, this book is a compilation of the hard lessons I've learned trading stocks through the years. Put simply, I focused on the things that work. I focused on the information you need to pay attention to so you can become a successful stock trader.

There are Tons of Investment Books Out There

Let's just get one thing out of the way, while it's true that this book is yet another of many stock investment books in the marketplace, most of those stock investment books have it all wrong. This book is intended to help newbie traders such as you to cut through the hype and fluff and get to the good stuff as quickly as possible.

You need to avoid my mistakes and benefit from what I got right. By getting the right information from the very beginning, you put yourself in a better position. You increase your chances of trading profitably, consistently. I can't emphasize the word "consistently" enough.

Make no mistake about it, anybody can get lucky from time to time. Unfortunately, luck is not going to put food on the table. Luck can fall short. You need a clear idea as to what works so you can trade with a higher chance of consistent profit.

Stock Trading is a Journey

I wish I could tell you that, just by reading this book, you will become a millionaire. Unfortunately, nobody can make that guarantee. You have to understand that stock trading is a journey.

Just like any trip, it involves growth. It involves changing your perspective and, yes, it involves overcoming challenges.

This book steps you through the jungle of confusing "stock market talk" and terms and puzzling "strategies." Instead, I explain strategies in clear, everyday English, so you can make truly informed decisions when looking for trading opportunities, timing your buying and selling, and reinvesting your profits.

I wish you the very best in your journey into the amazing and richly rewarding world of stock trading!

--------End of Preview---------

Preview of

Investing
For Beginners

Simple Investing Guide to Become an Intelligent Investor and Grow Your Wealth Continuously

By David Morales

Available on Amazon

https://www.amazon.com/dp//1546839704

https://www.amazon.co.uk/dp//1546839704

Introduction

If you're reading this book, you have some cash saved in the bank and you're thinking of growing your money. If this is the case, then you're definitely on the right track.

You are definitely on the right track because most people don't get to that stage. In fact, according to a recent survey, most Americans are living paycheck to paycheck. In fact, if they were forced to write a check for $2,000, half of America's households cannot cut that check. That's how bad things are when it comes to savings.

So if you have some cash saved in the bank and you are looking for ways to grow that pile of money, you are definitely on the right track. You are a responsible person, you are a forward thinker, and you have the raw ingredients to make that money work for you instead of you constantly having to work for your money.

The Bad News

Now for the bad news. Regardless of how much cash you may have saved, you need to grow your money because it is losing value every single day it sits in the bank. I know this is hard to believe because the $5,000 you have in your account still says $5,000 after several months sitting in the bank. When you check your statement, it says pretty much the same amount of money.

In fact, thanks to the interest being paid to you by the bank, it seems that your money is even growing by a small fraction. Well, don't get too excited. Every year, your money is able to buy less and less goods and services. This is called inflation.

Whatever your saved dollars can buy this year, will buy less next year. And it gets worse after that. In fact, the amount of products and services your money can buy on a year to year basis continues to go down. Unless you do something, your money won't be able to buy much of anything at a particular point in the future.

If you find this all hard to believe, keep in mind that in the 1930's, you could buy a house for $1,000. You could buy a car for a couple of hundred dollars. In fact, meals can be had for pennies. That's how much the US dollar has sunk in value over the decades.

Inflation is very much real and if you are not careful, the money that you worked so hard for to save up in the bank won't be able to do you much good, thanks to inflation. The worst part to all of this is that your money might deteriorate in value to such an extent that you would be putting yourself in a really tight spot at the point in your life where you are most vulnerable. I am of course talking about your retirement.

Do yourself a big favor and prepare for a better retirement future by deciding to simply get the most value out of the hard earned dollars you have stored away.

This book explores, in broad terms, *the different ways you can grow the value of the money that you have saved up*. This is money that you worked hard for. This is money that you sacrificed and sweated for. Make sure that it retains its value.

In fact, you should make sure that it grows in value over time instead of being eaten up by inflation. This book will not only open your mind to the prospect of increasing the value of your money, but hopefully get you excited about the whole investment process.

--------End of Preview---------